The **BIG** Jump

GCSE to A-levels

Ahmaan Immo

Contents

Introduction

Why Should YOU own this Guide?

A-levels, a nerve-wracking term teacher, older siblings, and even parents dart at the ears of y11 students. "it's a big jump" they say. "it's harder than A-levels" they say. But do they really tell you about how to overcome the leap from GCSE to A-Levels? Your teachers teach you Everything but the tools to tackle the jump and that's where this guide comes in handy. The 6-week summer holiday can be agonizing and confusing for many students as they pounder and contemplate over what's ahead whilst not knowing what's ahead and how to face it.

Containing over 70 pages I have compiled and gathered all the vital information you would ever need in order to enter y12 feeling like 'a million dollars.' In this guide, I provide you with the weapons you need to make the two-year-long journey ahead, as smooth as possible.

This guide covers EVERYTHING! From the leap between GCSE to A-levels to study techniques, effective revision methods, and how to probably revise to optimising revision in exam period. This is the lucid ENCYCLOPEDIA for you (Y10/Y11/12/13 students) enabling yourself to have a fascinating insight into what lies ahead. So, sit back relax, and allow me to prepare you for what the future holds.

What are A-levels?

Advanced Levels or A-Levels are subject-based qualifications that can lead to university, further study, training, or work.

A-Level courses are provided by Sixth Form Colleges and Further Education Colleges. In essence, these two institutions are the same except that Further Education Colleges operate separately from high schools, offer a wide variety of courses and qualifications, plus ensure a different more relaxed learning environment compared to high schools.

A-Levels are made up of AS levels and A2 levels.

AS levels can stand as a qualification on their own. However, it can be carried on to A2 the next year to complete the full qualification.

All A-level exams will take place at the end of Year 13, with no marks from AS levels contributing to the overall final grade.

AS assessments will typically take place after one year's study and A levels after two.

How are A-levels graded?

A-level grades range from E-A*, with A* being the highest,

The raw mark in papers are converted to marks on a Uniform Mark Scale (UMS) to give a comprehensive understanding of how well a student performed. If students achieve over 80% of UMS marks with an average of 90% across A2 modules they are awarded an A*

80-100% -- Grade A

70-79% -- Grade B

60-69% -- Grade C

50-59% -- Grade D

40-49% -- Grade E

Okay I understand, but what is UCAS???

UCAS stands for University and Colleges Admissions Services. An online system which enable you to apply to universities. Everyone who wants to study an undergraduate degree in the UK will have to apply through UCAS.

What is UCAS tariff?

The UCAS tariff assigns a value to each grade from A* to E for A levels

A* = 56 | A = 48 | B = 40 | C =32 | D =24 | E = 16

e.g. ABB - 128

And A-E for AS levels

A – 20| B – 16| C – 12| D – 10| E – 6

e.g. AAA - 60

How can I earn more UCAS points?

There are many ways in which you can achieve more UCAS points. The most popular ways are as follows:

Take an extra as level: - This can be a subject you enjoy and it doesn't need to have any connections with the other subjects and you have decided to take and the career path you would like to pursue (e.g. you want to go into medicine and you enjoy English literature) This will help boost your university application.

Taking EPQ: - Most sixth forms would provide the opportunity for you to take an EPQ. This is an additional qualification that can be taken alongside a-levels and is valued at 50% of a full a-level. Other than securing the opportunity for you to attend your dream university, it allows you to develop a significant number of vital skills.

Volunteering in your local community.

By taking an {ASDAN Community Volunteering Qualification students} can earn up to 16 UCAS points. These points can, in turn, be used towards a university application. This qualification is all about developing your volunteering skills and knowledge and recognising the unpaid work you do for the benefit of your community. It also enables you to stand out from the crowd when applying for university.

What subjects should you study for A-levels?

Even though I have advised you and your teachers have also advised you to take the subjects you enjoy it's important that you bear in mind the subjects that will give you the best chance when applying to university.

mandatory subjects required for different university courses:

- Most **Science subjects** at university (Medicine, Veterinary Science, Biology, Chemistry, Chemical Engineering, Biochemistry) require Chemistry. These subjects also require another science, many preferring Biology.

- For **Medicine and Veterinary Science**, it is best to take Chemistry, Biology, and one from either Maths or Physics. This way you will keep the vast majority of medical schools open to you.

- All **Language courses** at university require the language being studied and the top universities prefer a second language.

- Most **Engineering** courses require Maths and Physics

- Most **Economics courses** require Maths and certain universities like Further Maths (although they will rarely explicitly say so).

- Most **English** courses require English Literature – English Language on its own is not sufficient.

- **Humanities** courses such as History and Geography require that subject at A level.

- **Natural Sciences, Materials Science, Biomedical, Sciences, Environmental, Science, Optometry** and **Earth Sciences** (Geology) require two from Biology, Chemistry, Maths or Physics.

- Many **Sports Science** courses want to see one from Chemistry, Biology, Maths or Physics. Some may treat PE as a science.

- **Nursing and Midwifery** require Biology or another science.

- Leading **Psychology** courses request one from Chemistry, Biology, Maths or Physics.

- Most **Physiotherapy** courses will consider you with just Biology. However, many require a second science subject from Chemistry, Physics or Maths.

- Some **Architecture** courses want an arts and science mix. Many also ask for an art and design portfolio to demonstrate artistic skills so an Art or Design and technology A level may be critical.

- **Physics** courses require Physics and Maths.

- **Maths** courses require Maths and preferably Further Maths.

- **Actuarial Science** requires Maths

- **Accountancy** generally does not stipulate although one or two universities prefer Maths.

- Some **Management Studies** and **Computer Science** courses prefer Maths.

- Most traditional **Music** courses require Music and grade VII / VIII

- **Art & Design** courses require Art or Design Technology including AGCE/National.

- Some **Drama** courses require English Literature and for a few courses English and/or Theatre Studies.

- For **Classics** courses, Latin or Ancient Greek are required

- Some **Occupational Therapy** courses ask for Biology.

- In terms of **Teaching**, most A levels count. You need at least one from Art, Biology, Chemistry, Computing, Design and Technology, Drama (Theatre Studies), English, French, Geography, German, History, ICT, Italian, Mathematics, Music, Physics, Physical Education, Religious Studies (Theology) or Spanish.

- **Business Studies**, **Law**, **Anthropology**, **Archaeology**, **History of Art**, **Religious Studies**, **Politics**, **Philosophy**, **Sociology**, **Media studies,** and **Surveying** do not stipulate any mandatory A levels. Although some Law degrees and Media studies courses stipulate English.

3 or 4 A-levels?

Whilst the thought of taking 4 A-levels might please you, I am quite sure the extra workload won't. The time spent on taking another 'as or a-level' can be spent doing an EPQ and work experience which enables your personal statement to stand out to the universities you have applied for.

Taking 4 A-Levels might leave you with concerns that if you focused and dedicated your energy and time on only 3 A-Levels then you could have done yourself justice academically and would have achieved your full potential with three qualifications you are proud of.

No UK university asks for four A levels, and they understand that many students don't have the option to take more than three. Your offer will be based on 3 A-levels. This becomes an advantage for students TAKING 4 A- levels. Let's say the offer was A, A, A. The students will still receive their place in university even if they receive A, A, A, E.

A few other advantages to taking 4 A-Levels - enables students to have flexibility in which course they want to take in university. Even taking extra subjects just as an 'as' enables students to have an extra year to decide which three subjects they want to complete in full and which subject they want to drop.

You might also want to take 4-A-Levels when applying to Oxbridge to highlight your ingenuity. However, many students get into Oxbridge without 4 A-Levels so this isn't necessary.

YOU CAN FIND MORE ADVICE ON A-LEVELS AT
WWW.EDUMAP.ORG.UK

What subjects can you study for a-levels?

A

Accounting

Applied General

Art and Design

B

Bengali

Biology

Business

C

Chemistry

Chinese (Mandarin)

Citizenship Studies

Computer Science and IT

D

Dance

Design and Technology

Drama

E

Economics

Engineering

English

Entry Level Certificates (ELC)

EPQ

Entertainment Technology

F

Food

French

G

Geography

German

H

Hebrew (Biblical)

Hebrew (Modern)

History

History of Art

I

ICT

Italian

L

Languages

Law

M

Mathematics

Media Studies

Music

P

Panjabi

Performing Arts

Philosophy

Physical Education

Physics

Polish

Politics

Programmes

Projects

Psychology

Personal and Social Education

R

Religious Studies

S

Science

Sociology

Spanish

Statistics

T

Tech-levels

Technical Awards

U

Unit Award Scheme

Urdu

Easiest, Hardest, Most Popular and Least Popular A-Levels!

Easiest A-Levels

A-Level Law | Pass Rate- {96.2%} |No.5

Fairly easy to understand and doesn't require as much independent study as other A-Levels

A-Level Drama | Pass Rate- {99.2%} |No.4

A fun & engaging A-level that has a lot of content. Drama allows you to enjoy the experience of taking an A-level.

A-Level Film |Pass Rate- {99.2%} |No.3

Doesn't require huge amounts of effort and also enables you to enjoy the experience of doing an A-level. However, it doesn't give you a lot of options for other A-levels you can take.

A-Level Geography |Pass rate- {98.7%} |No.2

This A-level isn't content heavy and the content you are required to know is easy to learn and understand due to its fascinating nature.

A-Level Art |Pass Rate- {98.8%} |No.1

A very creative A-level which allows you to turn artistic imaginative notions into reality. This A-Level also comes with a fair bit of writing.

Hardest A-Levels

A-Level Computer Science | Pass Rate- {95.1%} | No.5
A challenging tough A-Level the requires you to memorise and learn about the computer right down to the tiniest detail. However, it's a prodigious essential skill that will increase the chance of your university application being accepted.

A-Level Biology | Pass Rate- {95.9%} | No.4

Around 3 times as hard as GCSE biology, this a level requires many rough hours of independent study. Another factor resulting into it being a difficult a level is the lack of resources. However, as this is a facilitating subject your path to university and employment will be smoother.

A-Level Chemistry | Pass Rate- {95.9%} | No.3

The hardest science you can take at A-level. This subject will push you to your limits and enable you to understand many fundamental aspects of life. Chemistry is usually referred to as the most important central science. This subject involves the memorization of complex concepts which could be hard at first but it's a great subject to have on your personal statement.

A-Level Further Maths | Pass Rate- {97.6%} | No.2

An insanely tricky content heavy subject that requires many hours of hard work. However, taking a-level further maths opens many doors for you in the employment world as its seen as an essential skill.

A-Level Modern Foreign Language | Pass Rate- {97.3%} | No.1
e.g. French, mandarin, Spanish and German. Any language takes many tiring hours of hard work to master and perfect. However, if you look on the bright side after two years you would have developed many cognitive skills and would have learn about a different culture ultimately strengthening your brain muscles and creates job security. It also makes travel a lot easier and allows you to swear in a different language which is always an advantage so there is no reason to be scared of it just because it ranks the highest in the list.

15

10 Most Popular Subjects	10 Least Popular Subjects
• Maths • Biology • Psychology • Chemistry • History • English Literature • Art and Design subjects • Physics • Sociology • Geography	• Communication And Culture • Archaeology • Electronics • Health & Social Care (double award) • Anthropology • History Of Art (western world) • Bengali • Classical Civilisation • Environmental studies • Modern Hebrew

The differences and similarities between GCSE and A-levels

The differences and similarities between GCSE and A-levels

The jump between GCSE and A-levels would probably be the biggest jump in your education. Every A-level is equivalent to 6 GCSE's so taking 3 A-Levels would be like taking 18 GCSE. But is this the real reason why people fail to conquer a-levels?

Well certainly not, if you plan ahead the 2 years should be adequate time for you to go over all the content and be prepared but it's the revision methods people use. Due to your success with a certain revision method for GCSE's doesn't mean it will be effective for A-levels. This is the reason why many students are dragged down into the deep trenches of D'S and E's.

The workload – one of the many things that hijack students' chance of receiving that A or A*. The workload is guaranteed to become more intense and stressful and will require a significant amount of your time to complete. But remember its manageable if you are determined to succeed. However, if your one of those students who coasted through their GCSE then it's vital that you change your approach to your studies. To manage the workload all you have to do is deploy a timetable from early 12 that requires you to stay on top of what has been taught every day in your classes.

How important is self-discipline? --- As you could imagine very important! Self-discipline is self-control, inner strength, authority over yourself. This is a crucial skill that enables you to not just be productive but also successful as you're able to guide yourself to accomplish what is needed of you to accomplish. It's a vital skill for all students, it's the ability to not snooze your alarm in the hazy morning, it's the ability to turn of money heist to go to your room and cementing your backside to the choking chair for hours gazing blindly at your never-ending notes, it's the ability to want to succeed and acting on it.

So how do I achieve that self-discipline? First and foremost, you need to identify your strength and weaknesses. Your weakness might be your love for watching study tubers and not acting upon the ideas and methods of revision they convey to you. Your weakness might be your obsession with winning the one v one in the gulag. Whatever it is you need to identify your problem to conquer it. You need to be aware of your downfalls to avoid falling agonisingly into the same treacherous pits. Not everyone is perfect so when you do fall into these pits get up. Don't lose hope. Stand up and challenge yourself to get better. In all honesty, I found my self-discipline through waking up early even though lately, COVID-19 has been my excuses, waking up early for the last 2 years has enabled me to not just be more productive, and can complete vital tasks at a much faster pace without being distracted but it has also given me an inner pleasure and that amazing start to my day which ultimately makes me think I'm ahead of others. An overdose of this arrogance can be very unhealthy but it's vital to have a bit of confidence that allows you to ultimately have happier more fruitful days.

A-levels enable you to shine a light on your creativity, passion, and craving for a certain subject. E.g. you might be passionate about French due to it being filled with rich elegant vocabulary and sounding words. You might think and believe that knowing a language like French is key to facilitating communication between countries. You might be interested to see the world through the eyes of a French speaker or learn about their culture, traditions, and history. These interests could be your willpower to sit hours and hours without getting tired.

How to prepare for your a-levels in the summer!

*Strengthen your foundation (GCSE) before September—Especially for languages as abandoning the vocab you have learned for six weeks could stress you out at the beginning of y12 as you would have to relearn them. This doesn't require hardcore revision. A quick glance over all the topics you have studied in y10/11 should give you the head start you need. Don't stress yourself and work at your own pace.

Read around the subject? / watch movies- even though I was throwing shade at money heist but it could help reading the subtitles and getting used to the pronunciation of certain Spanish words if your planning on studying Spanish as an A-level. Reading around the subject is vital for later on when you are scripting your personal statement.

PDF FOR WIDER READING / GENERAL RESOURCES:

http://www.highdown.reading.sch.uk/_site/data/files/documents/D45C34 A4EC2AE527DED50C08324D03D2.pdf

Get as many resources as you can, the endorsed textbook and revision guide should be your starting point. YouTube is a great platform to find free resources that can assist you in the two years ahead.

Get organised. Upgrading your stationery can help you to plan for the more intense level of study and adapt to the level of organisation you'll need as an A-Level student. Printing the syllabus for each subject is vital when it comes to a-levels. It helps you track your progress and makes sure that you have covered all the content required for you to know to be prepared for the exam.

Note the ideas and concepts you could have implemented or things you could have done better when revising for your GCSE's. Try to implement the things you have written down when revising for your A-levels, reflect, and improve.

Know how you want to revise (I go through this later on in the guide) flashcards and mind maps are vital when it comes to a-levels so learn how to make them (more info on pg. 43,47)

Know what you're facing. e.g. maths- confusing concepts, so what could you do to overcome this?
You could get a grip on trigonometry and algebra. you need to be able to do these without having to think.
Get a better calculator (Casio FX-991ES plus or the Sharp EL-W506)

English lit - workload and unusual vocabulary. so, what could you do to overcome this?

Be prepared for what you're facing - reading books in advance, the context, and about the author's life to have a better understanding. I am not asking you to start analysing but what I am asking is for you to give your brain a jumpstart a head start to make the path ahead trouble-free.

Priorities relaxation - enjoy yourself, don't try to get ahead and overstress yourself. Remember as much as you need to work, you also need some chill time. If you do this by the time sixth form/college starts in September, you'll actually enjoy studying resulting into better focus in class and at home ultimately elevating your grades.

Revision preparation

Before we indulge in the depth details of different revision methods and how it can excel you to excellent grades, you and I need to ask ourselves one simple yet requisite question, Why revise? Why spend your valuable time snapping your backbone, slanting your stiff, sore neck, and allowing your soul to be engulfed by a revision guide? Why?

To help you answer this odd yet crucial question, I will outline a few motivations, a few reasons, a few ways to make an agreement with yourself that you have a reason to revise. Some of you reading this might assume I'm just trying to fill white space and the only reason you should revise is so you can pass the exam. But will that give you enough motivation, enough drive, enough determination to excel in your studies? As I said many times before and, in this guide, motivation has the ability to jump-start you for a few hours, minutes, seconds but discipline is what will be your driving force to success. But this doesn't mean motivation will not play its part. You need to be motivated to be disciplined. And this is where Long- and short-term goals come into place.

So, what do we mean by long term goals and what can it be?

Long term goals can be anything regarding your future career or even your educational goals. For a certain student, this might be going to Cambridge and for another, it might be having a successful career in medicine. Whatever it might be, it's the idea of having something a few miles ahead of you that can motivate your tyres i.e. your legs, your brain, and in general your whole body every morning to keep rolling.

A short-term goal is something that you want to achieve and complete in the near future. This can be just about anything, from getting the highest grade in the monthly maths exams to doing 9 hours of revision today. The speedy accomplishment it gives you can be a big driving force for your engine to keep functioning.

It helps 'minimalise procrastination and maximise productivity' (our revision period motto). Saying to yourself 'I'll revise for 3 hrs every day' will push you to the defined path to success and getting an A rather than just saying I want an A and hoping something magical happens with the results of next year's exams. Short term goals are what make you achieve long-term goals

Short Term Goals+ Short Term Goals = Long Term Goal

Now that we understand why we are revising and the importance of having a goal to look forward to, we can move on to some general revision tips to lay down the foundation as I help you, the builders, with constructing your own mansions with the many scientifically proven effective revision methods.

- **Establishing your note-taking system** – this is a vital step when it comes to having structure within your revision. You should develop your own note-taking system based on your learning preference. (More info pg.)

- **Active vs passive revision** - Passive revision is the one most people prefer doing and it comprises of activities such as reading and constructing notes. Whilst making 'Peng' notes is a crucial aspect of your revision journey, it will not help you in any way pass your exams. This is where active revision comes in. It is more focused on using the material you have accumulated and actually understanding it to have the ability to recall it later on (pg.___)

- **Sleep solidifies memory** - Oxbridge in an article state that studies have shown the correlation between quality steep and solid memory. Pulling ''all-nighters' can have a big bad impact on your result. The phrase 'let me sleep on it' indicates that a good night's sleep can do wonders when it comes to arranging and storing information in our brains.

- **Meditation can stimulate improvement of memory** - mediation aids to build awareness of your thoughts, emotions/feelings. It has just been over a month since I have started meditating (when writing this book) and so far, I have encountered many benefits. Just like going to the gym, it doesn't show massive results immediately but builds your mental and spiritual strength gradually. And it only requires just 5-10 minutes a day. Meditation doesn't only improve visualisation skills and concentration skills but it's also a great method for relaxation (perfect before an exam).

- **Take breaks** – A-levels are very content heavy and can be a confusingly dark dismal dreary alleyway when you first enter it. You might want to do a myriad number of hours of work daily but this will just make you feel miserable about the subjects you have chosen thus causing you to burn out. So, find your balance and stick to it.

There are 4 main different learning styles that suit 4 different types of learns!

1) Visual Learners - These are students who learn through observing physical space. How would you know if you're a visual learner, well you would have a preference for learning through seeing or observing this, including pictures, diagrams, written directions and more? Visual learners usually take more time to process the material. so, make sure to give yourself the time and space to work through the information.

2) Auditory Learners – These students acquire knowledge better when it in the form of sound. They would prefer to listen to lectures rather than read notes. Hearing their e.g. notes in audio form aids them to relieve stress, organise their thoughts, and understand the concept with much more clarity and detail. This is you if you are the student in your class that likes to engage, share ideas, read out loud, and verbally explain concepts (better) than when writing it down.

3) Kinesthetic learners – These students learn and revise best through movement-based activities such as role-play. To them, notes/ theory of a concept doesn't please them until it is put into practice so they can witness the outcome of what the knowledge they have assimilated. These are the students who might struggle to sit for long periods and might be good at sports or dance. They usually can't revise for long periods and have messy handwriting.

4) Linguistic Learners – Fleming and Mills in 1992 stated in their VARK Modalities theory that reading/writing learners prefer to learn through written words. This does over lapse with visual learners. These students tend to 'thinking in words. They can read volumes and synthesise all of it in the exam. These are the students who prefer to remember certain concepts in creative ways such as by using mnemonics.

The benefits of starting revision early!

Drilling our fingers into our eyes we put our feet to the ground. Jabbing the alarm OFF and making our way to our second office. We get ready for the day ahead, put clothes on, and attend school. Our battery percentage drops to 20% on our way back as it suddenly shifts into the 6th gear accelerating its way to zilch. arriving home, we suddenly collapsing onto our bed, we find ourselves magically scrolling on Instagram under our duvet. Whining BS with a feeble voice we say to ourselves "I'm going to revise tomorrow".

This page is dedicated to supplying you with the medications needed to cure this ubiquitous disease.

Why start revising early when I can just cram it?

- **Avoiding Stress** – One of the best feelings a student can experience isn't cracking a funny joke and being well-regarded by his class peers but it's being prepared for an upcoming exam. The reassurance, comfort, and self-confidence it gives you are infinite. You get to also sleep the night before the exam which is a bonus.

- **Time to perfect exam techniques** – The famous maxim "life is unfair" applies to the exams. Receiving a Grade 9 or an A* in A-levels doesn't define you as smart but flexible. Being well-spoken and writing isn't going to give you the ticket to a grade 9 in English and that's what I try and address in my other guides. Exams are designated to trick and blur you but you need to focus your lens and be aware of where the potholes are so you don't accidentally fall into them. We are all aware of the saying "practice makes perfect". Use and train the god gifted Waze in your brain with the locations of these potholes. This will enable you to get to the other side of the exam having defeated it. There's a myriad number of exam practice papers to download for all subjects and inject into your revision timetable. So why not! Be prepared so you don't enter the exam impaired.

- **Organisation** – Preparation is key as we have stated previously and the finest method of preparing for success is being organised early on. Understanding what your reading. Making and remaking notes is crucial. Taking practice papers and grading can have a drastic impact on raising your grades. Get organised early on, create a timetable(pg._) and avoid leaving potholes in your knowledge.

Revision Methods with Scientific evidence

Active recall / spaced repetition

Some of us have dashed our way past the first fewer barriers of revision which are things such as having the discipline and having long/short term goals. You are willing to spend hours revising, memorising and cohering knowledge only for you to forget it all a day later. The forgetting curve hypothesizes the decline in memory, of what we have encountered, overtime at an exponential rate.

So, what's the solution to this?

Active recall (quizzing, testing) is the process by which we challenge our minds to retrieve information rather than passively reviewing/ re-reading the same thing and failing to recall it.

After making pages and pages of glittering yellow-painted notes, you might think to yourself that you would remember what you have encountered. This is not the case, reading the same notes a myriad number of times, could help you remember it but Researchers have proven active recall to be significantly less time consuming and more effective. This technique married with spaced repetition will help to stretch and expand your ability to recall information in the long term.

Spaced repetition is the idea of distributing the active recall of learned concepts over time. You allow your brain to forget some of the information to ensure the active recall process is mentally strenuous. The physiology literature suggests that the harder your brain has to work to retrieve and decode certain information, the longer it would remember it.

You might want a less stressful but impactful method of remembering information faster due to you abhorring quizzes and tests. Well as a more everyday alternative, you could employ a deceptively simple technique known as cloze deletion (A fancy 'oo, look at me' way of saying fill in the blank). A salient keyword/phrase It's concealed from the passage which in essence challenges your brain to recall the certain missing word/phrase. It requires your brain searching for an answer and as we said previously 'the harder your brain has to work to retrieve and decode certain information, the longer it would remember it.'

Active recall and spaced repetition are the two legs of the chair known as memory. You are allowed to attach information to this chair to cheat from it come exam time.

The idea isn't to memorise large blocks of futile text but it is to be able to identify and reprogram your brain create a chain and spot patterns to connects certain pieces of information to others.

Spaced repetition can be useful when revising topics, you haven't learnt over days and weeks but also reviewing it on the same day. Let's assume this morning you learnt surds and algebraic equations. Before moving onto other topics that same afternoon, you could do a quiz or even deploy the methods of cloze depletion to recall and put the information that you have acquired deeper into your memory.

Active recall+ spaced revision is considered by many to be the best revision method. It has much evidence and research supporting it. It aids to keep your mind fresh, relaxing the mind can help you to remember what it needs to remember. Trying to remember what you wrote under the image on pg. 52 of your notes can results in anxiety, pressure, and stress during the exam. This method is far more enhanced and effective compared to the usual spilling yellow dye on your notes.

Metacognition

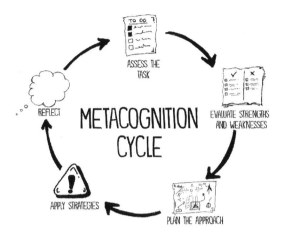

Metacognition is being aware of your thought process. The key difference between an average student and a successful one is the ability to not just known about metacognition but to exercise it. Metacognition is merely thinking about our thinking. Research indicates that the ability to critically analyse how we think influences our approach task and what strategies we deploy to solve the problem we face. It enables us to identify the gaps in our knowledge but also the strengths and weaknesses in order to make amendments to our tactic and maximise productivity.

The process can be portrayed in a cycle containing five main steps:

1) **Assessing** the task ahead

2) **Evaluate strengths and weaknesses**, to understand what you need to have or know to overcome this task

3) **Plan** - A very vital stage of the cycle, it helps to visualise everything. This plan doesn't have to be detailed or aesthetic.

4) **Applying strategies and monitoring the effectiveness** of these strategies.

5) **Reflect how effective the plan has been** – this can lead to your strategy being adjusted for it to be more effective leading to you having to assess the task again—and the cycle repeats

Benefits of Following the Metacognition Cycle

- *It helps us to identify our strengths and weaknesses and make amendments to our approach accordingly thus increasing productivity.

- *"What am I trying to achieve?" "Am I on the right track?" "How can I improve my approach?" -- You will begin to notice that by reflecting on your progress, you become more motivated to achieve your study goals!

- *Summoning your prior knowledge-- Answering these questions will give context to what you are learning and help you start building a framework for new knowledge.

- *Think aloud-- a great way to test yourself as you exercising your hippocampus to actively recall information.

- *Take notes from memory--help you identify what you do and don't know.

- *Organize your thoughts--visualize material, this helps connect between the various concepts you are learning. Creating a mind map from memory is also a great study strategy because it is a form of self-testing.

Mind map

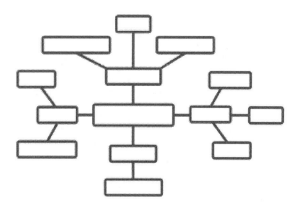

A mind map is a simple diagram you make with lots of branches demonstrating related ideas.

Mind maps are an outstanding revision method as it has direct links to active recall & spaced repetition. It's also a remarkable method when you want to summarise or get a synoptic view of a topic or a whole course. It's vital to understand the chains and links between different concepts and sections of your course especially at A-level and mind maps make that possible.

History of mind maps

Visual representations of information have been used for thousands of years. The term "mind map", however, wasn't around until the 1970s, when it was coined by the English researcher Tony Buzan. Buzan was searching for a way to deal with the large amounts of information he needed to memorize during his time at university. He studied the notes of the greatest thinkers he could find and combined their approaches with his own research about psychology, creative thinking, and memorization. Eventually, after the first successes with his newly developed technique, he started writing a series of books on the subject.

Making effective Mind maps

- **Effectively maximise productive in your study time** - Students that make better use of their time are the ones that have good time management skills and also discipline. You become more organised, confident, and productive as you learn more effectively in a shorter period of time. Mapping out a revision timetable can be the door to opening your productivity. It's vital to have some sort of plan, it doesn't just keep you disciplined but it also ensures that you have done the work and gives you a sense of reassurance and confidence. – (www.edumap.org.uk For FREE Online Mind Mapping + ready-made templates)

- **Stop overloading yourself with information** - People are often exposed to more information than they can remember. Despite this frequent form of information overload, little is known about how much information people can understand and retain. Mind maps can prevent this information overload allowing you to write a keyword/phrase per branch resulting in pages and pages of notes condensed into a single sheet. Having clear visual resources aids to manage the vast amount of information you exposed to and are required to understand.

- Make your mind maps interactive/having the main concept- To begin with, you'll need the main concept for your mind map that can birth different branches with valuable information regarding that main concept. Without the main concept mind maps are useless as the whole point of a mind map is to make revision more effective. Colour enables you to enjoy revision to a certain extent as your notes are alive and entertaining to read and revise from. Scientific studies have also proven that the use of colour helps to improve your ability to recall and remember information.

Pomodoro Technique

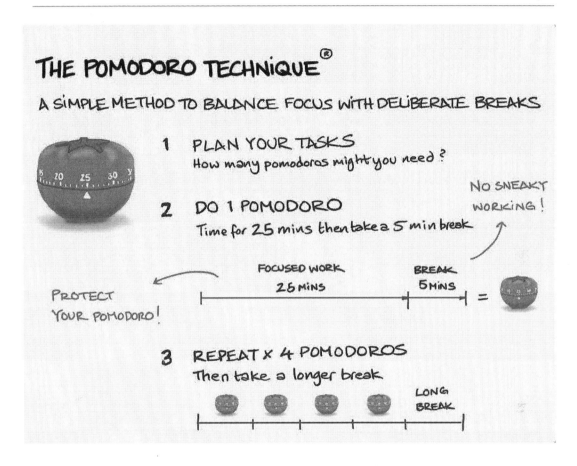

The Pomodoro Technique is a simple yet effective time management methodology that enables you to improve your focus. Developed by Francesco Cirillo in the late 1980s, this technique allows a user to choose a task and focus on it for 25-minute intervals. Pomodoro is the Italian word for tomato. Francesco Cirillo was a university student at the time and used a tomato timer to measure the 25-minute intervals.

This technique ties in with the famous Parkinson's law that "Work expands so as to fill the time available for its completion". The Pomodoro technique makes great use of this law as it helps us utilise our valuable time whilst improving the quality and quantity of work, we can produce over 24hrs.

How does this technique work?

- **Choose a task** you want to complete. This can be anything, from next week's homework to an email you were putting off for a decade. Any task big or small.

- **Focus** and get prepared to make use of your time in a productive manner. Close all your social media, close the door, turn off the music, and start social distancing from your phone. Remember its only 25 minutes till you can like one of my Instagram photos {so be patient}. Get into the right zone and tell yourself in a loud proud voice "You can do this".

- **Set the timer** for only 25 minutes, make your mind leave this world, and fully dive into whatever your revising. Don't go for a drink, toilet break, or even a cheeky chat with a family member. Just revise.

- After completing 25 minutes of productive work, step away from your desk, and allow your mind to clear for 5 minutes (**Short Break**). It's up to you whether you go on twitter, meditate or get yourself a cosy cup of coffee, whatever you do just relax and allow yourself to feel refreshed for another 25 minutes of productivity

The cycle repeats

- After a couple of sessions (4-5) give yourself a **longer break** to enable your brain to relax and get prepared for more productive Pomodoro sessions.

Why you may choose 3-5-hour blocks over the Pomodoro technique:

- Maximise productivity

- Minimise breaks

- Increase free time

- Maximise efficiency

How to Prepare to study in 3-5 hr blocks

- Plan the night before – quick to-do list

- Get everything you need before starting to study

- Social distance from your phone (2m to stop the spread of unproductivity)

- Give yourself rewards

- Have discipline e.g. (Even if you really need that cup of coffee, tell yourself 'you'll only get it after 2hrs')

To conclude, this technique can change your whole dynamic on approaching revision. It can help organise your time and change 'time' from being an alarming infuriating enemy to being an ally that helps us keep on top of everything to achieve success. Whilst having done so much work, you wouldn't feel burnt out and exhausted because throughout your revision you were rewarding and refreshing yourself with constant breaks to relax. All you need to implement this fantastic technique that has the power to revolute your whole revision journey is a timer, paper, and pencil.

Flashcards

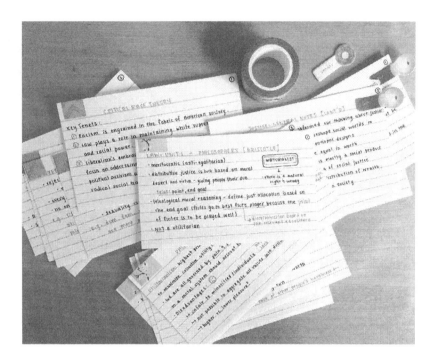

Flashcards are a classic simple study tool. It is a set of small, double-sided cards used to learn and revise details and install active recall within your revision. You look at the front side(question) of the flashcard and think of the answer, by doing this you are implementing active recall. You are challenging your brain to remember a certain concept you have come across thus making the concept stick stiffer into your brain.

How To Make Effective Flash Cards?

1. Make use of both sides of the flashcard. One containing a question or a key term to quiz your brain and the other containing the answer or definition of the key term. Remember it's not a notebook, it's called a flashcard for a reason, simplify your existing notes into the most significant information.

2. Your goal isn't to bombard one flashcard with much different vital information. Ensure that you keep each idea on its own flashcard. Split longer complex concepts over several flashcards to make it easier for your brain to recall. You might end up with more flashcards but your revision will certainly be more effective

3. Flashcards utilises your metacognitive faculties- You don't want your exam to be the first time you accurately assess how well you know the material. Self-testing should be an integral part of your study sessions so that you have a clear understanding of what you do and don't know. Flashcards authorise you to prepare the different pieces of your brain to answer questions based on the knowledge you have acquired. After completing a set of flashcards, you are essentially questioning yourself "How did my answer compare to this correct answer" and "How well did I know (or not know it)". This act of self-reflection is what is known as metacognition.

4. Used spaced repetition- As I stated in pg.31-33 Active recall & spaced repetition is the most potent and effective revision method and flashcards are one of the many study methods that prove this. Flashcards are a great method to test yourself quickly and conveniently. Spaced repetition is the technique of testing yourself several times at different intervals. The Ebbinghaus forgetting curve illustrates the decrease in the ability for your brain to maintain memory over time therefore, making it vital that we revisit the flashcards that we have created several times.

5. Flashcards are a prodigious revision method but to make your revision as productive and efficient as it can be, I'd recommend you implement another technique such as quizzes (past papers) or mind maps- (To create customised virtual mind maps visit my website www.edumap.org.uk)

Feynman Technique

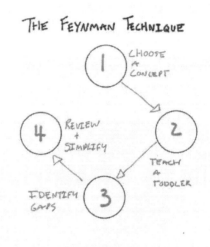

The Feynman Technique is a mental model named after Richard Feynman, a Nobel prize-winning physicist. Known as the 'Great Explainer,' Feynman had the ability to explain complicated concepts in simple terms and illustrations. The idea behind this technique is to pinpoint any foggy areas in your knowledge so you can deploy your windshield wipers to improve your sight. The technique has helped millions of students around the world retain and understand the information they have learnt.

This technique doesn't just transform your revision time to be more effective and productive but it also makes it way less tedious and dreary. This technique involves taking breaks from going through your notes and attempting to understand the information you have read

1. **Write down the concept you want to learn** - Take a blank piece of paper and write the name of the concept at the top. This can be anything but the more specific the better.

2. **Teach and depict the concept in your own words** - Explain it as if you were teaching It to someone else (precisely an 8-year-old). Use plain understandable English that can be understood by anyone. This stage of the process should allow you to pinpoint what you don't quite know. Challenge yourself to work through a few examples regarding the concept to fully assure yourself that you understand the concept

3. **Review your explanation** of the complex and pinpoint the gaps in your knowledge (where your explanation feels wobbly) and areas where you used complex language. Go back to either your notes or course material and attempt to get a better understanding of your weaker areas.

4. **Re-write the wobbly parts** of your explanation again in simpler terms.

Feynman Technique is all about keeping it simple. With Feynman's method, you can trim down all of the extra study time to just the basics and learn to grasp, understand, and recall the lesson's key concepts.

There are two types of knowledge and most of us focus on the wrong one. The first type of knowledge focuses on knowing the name of something. The second focuses on knowing something.

These are not the same thing. The famous Nobel winning physicist Richard Feynman understood the difference between knowing something and knowing the name of something and it's one of the most important reasons for his success.

"The person who says he knows what he thinks but cannot express it usually doesn't know what he thinks."- Mortimer Adler

The Cornell Method?

There are countless note-taking techniques that you could adapt to in your revision. Personally, I have never tried the Cornell note-taking method but due to its extreme popularity, I thought it would be vital for me to go through how to efficiently use this method.

This Cornell note-taking method was devised in the 1950s by DR. Walter Paulk of Cornell University. He developed a method that actively improves your study skills and makes reviewing your notes more effective and time-efficient, crucial when preparing for an exam.

How to take notes using the Cornell note-taking method

1. Segment your page into 3 sections- Draw a horizontal line across the bottom portion of your page (Later you will be using this section to summarise your notes). Draw a vertical line down the left section of your paper – (approx. 2.5inches from the left edge of the paper – section for reviewing notes). Leave the largest section of the page to take notes from the lecture/class.

2. Start writing in the notes Column – record key words, ideas, facts, charts, formulas, and case studies. Don't bombard yourself with useless information.

3. Formulate questions based on the notes that you have compiled and written them in the left column. These can be effective when trying to implement active recall into your revision.

4. Write a brief summary of all the notes in the summary section. This section will be vital later on in exam season when you're trying to quickly go through the main key ideas of each topic.

Advantages	Disadvantages
<ul><li>Can be written in any format **e.g.** add a diagram</li><li>Neat/aesthetic note-taking method</li><li>Easy to create a template for typed notes</li><li>Effective and efficient in exam season and when revising over content-heavy topics</li></ul>	<ul><li>Limit space- hard to fit all the notes on one page</li><li>Time-consuming note-taking method</li><li>Maybe difficult to fit all the sections of the page</li><li>Quite a boring note-taking method</li></ul>

Past papers & Mark schemes

The most strenuous and underrated revision and exam preparation method. You might strongly believe that there's nothing more sickening and horrifying to look at then a pile of freshly printed past papers. But when you understand the benefit of these papered creatures and the impact it can have on your final grade, you will begin to love them, treasure them and insert them into your revision schedule.

A great analogy that can get you started is that you wouldn't prepare for a basketball game by social distancing from basketball. Same thing here, you can't prepare for an exam without coming into contact and practicing past papers and understanding its direct proportion to you attaining a high grade in the exam.

Using Past Papers & Mark Schemes Efficiently!

1. Practice questions- Once you have acquired all the notes you will need; you must dive straight into one of the most useful revision strategies when preparing for an exam. Completing practice questions. This offers a sense of achievement and boost in confidence. It allows you to identify any gaps in your knowledge and enables you to actively recall information which is pivotal when training your brain to remember a certain piece of information.

2. Understand the significance of exam conditions:

3. Colour code your practice paper:

> Red = questions you cannot attempt at all
>
> Orange = questions you are can attempt, but are not confident with

> Exam Conditions:
>
> ✓ No internet
> ✓ No notes
> ✓ Isolated room
> ✓ No breaks
> ✓ Nothing else on desk other than black or blue pen

4. Go through the examiner report as it's filled with vital information and exam techniques. the people who are going to mark your exams have written this document. Utilise it. Print it out and highlight the key points.

Finally, Mark the paper yourself but be strict. the examiner doesn't know what's going on in your head. don't deceive yourself by rewarding yourself extra marks.

Blurting

Blurting might sound like a technique that requires you to vomit, but it's not. It's far from being barf and repulsive as its one of the most effective efficient revision techniques I have ever come across.

Blurting is a technique likened to mind mapping but without the elegance. You write the title of the topic in the middle of a blank paper and note down everything concerning that topic that you can think of from the top of your head. You then go back to your notes to identify the potholes and distinguish what is in your long and what is in your short-term memory. You fill them in on your paper but in a different colour to make them stand out.

This technique can be done both written and verbally. Doing it verbally would require you to time yourself for 5 minutes and state everything you know about that topic. After the time is up, you will check your notes to highlight the pieces of information that you have missed out.

Spaced repetition is vital when trying to maximise the benefits out of this technique. Blurt the same topic a week after your first blurt. This will help to reinforce and further cement the knowledge into your brain.

Other General Revision Methods! This is a list of alternatives, quite thought-provoking revision techniques that you can implement into your preparation for your exams.

1. **Rapping it** - Yes, you might not just yet be of a similar skill level as the like of Dave & Jay-z, but compiling a few sentences and making them memorable through the use of rhyme can help glue valuable information into your brain.

2. **Make some memes** - A form of revision which is way easier to adhere to. Go on a website that enables you to create memes for free and turn every problematic concept into a memorable joke.

3. **Test Your Friend** - Everyone loves a good old quiz so compile a few questions and tell your friend to do the same. Or an alternative would be to get your sibling/family member to test you.

4. **Post-it notes** - Repaint your house with these. imprison all the walls of your house with different coloured post-it notes. These act as a reminder as you're constantly seeing these whilst watching tv, in the bathroom, or when your just about to sleep and so you will not forget the most essential information.

5. **Make PowerPoint Presentations** - This can tie into one of the effective techniques that we have discussed previously: (Feynman Technique). Use creative pictures, Gifs, and transitions to make your PowerPoint really engaging. Whilst your typing, you're re-reading the information in your head and this is a form of revision. You could also present the PowerPoint to a younger member of the family through the Feynman Technique.

6. **YouTube** is a very useful resource when it comes to revising. There are a vast number of free resources that you can utilise and implement into your revision. However, you have to contrast the positives and negatives of YouTube as it's also a great distraction. You will be watching a free science lesson video and the next thing you know you're watching paint dry (ASMR version). This is where having discipline becomes convenient.

In summary, it doesn't matter which study technique/ method you practice, the main aim is to revise and revise effectively. The three main revision techniques everyone needs to vaccinate into their revision schedule are active recall, spaced repetition, and past papers. These are the three main edges to the knife that you will need to defeat the gruesome, petrifying, daunting dreadful pile of revolting papers known as the exam.

The benefits of sleeping early

Waking up early! One of the most strenuous, gruelling punishments we can think of. transporting from the warmth of our beds to the harshness and grimness of reality. This thought is bound to send shivers down our spine and cause us to whisper to ourselves "I'll start my journey to productivity tomorrow".

Maybe sleeping just an hour or two early can help fight the cosy loving demon inside you and give you the ability to acquire the discipline you need to reach the goals you desire.

"The two most important days in your life are the day you are born and the day you find out why"

You need to have a goal ahead of you. One that can bounce your ass of the bed and demand you to working hard to achieve it. Your ears and eyes have probably previously been obliterated with this quote but I'll mention it here due to its significance.

"Every morning you have two options. Continue to sleep with your dreams or wake up and chase them."

There are many benefits of sleeping early and waking up early. This consists of improved memory, increased creativity, sharper attention, and most importantly, sleeping early has a direct correlation to improved grades (Not causation).

As well as resting your body, sleep primes the brain form new memories when you wake up. Try this, before you sleep read your notes on a certain topic and when you wake up, test yourself. You will see a quick increase in your ability to recall your notes. sleep lets us soak new memories/knowledge in so they'll stay there for the long-term.

Whilst we sleep, our brain replays the memories and the information we have encountered. This process is thought to by many scientists the result for the strengthening of information during sleep.

A study on the effect of sleep deprivation on cognitive performance found that "total sleep deprivation impairs attention and working memory, but it also affects other functions such as long-term memory and decision-making", "Partial sleep deprivation is found to influence attention, especially vigilance". This study highlights how salient it is to sleep and sleep for the ideal number of hours (7-10 depending on age).

At the end of the day, it's your choice. Sleeping is a beneficial legal drug. It's vital to your life but an overdose cannot just make you feel 'droopy' but it can also hamper your ability to be productive throughout the day and accomplish the many short term goals in your path needed to be accomplished to stretch yourself to seize your long term goal.

The power of a To-Do List

You might, at this stage of reading the book, understand what you have to do to maximise your time and the myriad number of different effective techniques but are unaware of how you can get yourself to implement this. As much as it's imperative to have the discipline to help you focus on your goal blindly, employing a to-do list can help to stay on top of everything.

Psychologist and author Dr. David Cohen believe his struggle to stay organised is helped immensely by a to-do list. "my family thinks I'm chaotic" he states in a guardian interview. He puts his love of to-do lists down to three reasons:

- They dampen anxiety about the chaos of life;
- They give us a structure, a plan that we can abide by;
- Proof of achievement giving you a sense of accomplishment

A lack of a to-do list (a planned structure to your day) can hurt your ability to be productive and have good time management. To-do lists enable you to move from one task to another without wasting time debating what to do next, making you as Levitin (Author of 'The organized mind') says 'the ultimate productive ninja'.

Roy Baumeister and EJ Masicampo at Florida State University were interested in an old phenomenon called the Zeigarnik Effect, which is what psychologists call our mind's tendency to get fixated on unfinished tasks and forget those we've completed.

The so-called "Zeigarnik effect"– stemmed from observing that waiters could only recall diners' orders before they had been served. After the dishes had been delivered, their memories simply erased who'd had the steak and who'd had the soup. The deed was done and the brain was ready to let go.

"Before you eat the elephant, make sure you know what parts you want to eat."

Creating an effective To-Do list

1. **Choose your platform** - have one system in place. E.g. notebook, bullet journal, or an app on your phone or computer. If you're someone who is always carrying around a notebook then make your to-do list on there. However, if you're like me and is obsessed with technology and always has a device around them, then you can create your to-do list on there.

   Top 5 To-do list apps: Todoist | Google Keep | TickTick | Microsoft todo | ClickUp |

2. **Consistency** - The transition from being a lazy 'wasteman' to a productive guru isn't going to happen over time. But being consistent and completing as many tasks on the list will aid you to get closer to that aim. Create a routine so that maintenance tasks can run on autopilot.

3. **Find your balance and be realistic** - To achieve your dream you need a plan, you need steps, you need short term goals, you need a to-do list. But it's vital that you are careful when crafting one. We as homo sapiens tend to be over-ambitious at times when we have a boost in motivation so planning on revising/other productive tasks 17 hrs a day, 7days a week is very unrealistic and unhealthy which could result into a burnout.

Don't include more than 8 items on the list because you are less likely to get it done and it can be more daunting the longer it is. Our plan is to be productive in the long term and have a big impact on our time management in the long term and the best way to achieve this is by setting a realistic to-do list from the beginning.

'This act of planning (to-do lists) reduces the burden on the brain, which is struggling to hold the mental list of all the things we have to do. Releasing the burden of unfinished tasks on the mind frees it up to become more effective.'

Improving your to-do list:

1. **Time-blocking** - Assigning individual tasks to manageable time slots.

2. **If / Then lists** - Making two lists. One for high energy days where you are bound to be more productive and one for your weary days. A bullet journal enthusiast by the name of Kara Benz suggests that both lists should follow an if/then model. E.g." If I have a lot of energy, then I'll take a walk at lunch". The second list would consist of tasks that are useful but require less brain power e.g. organising your desk.

3. **The Ivy Lee Method** - This productive hack transformed how tasks were organised back in 1918 but it is still very effective and useful. Taking 10-15 minutes at the end of the day writing down only 6 tasks that you would like to complete tomorrow and prioritize them out of importance. Focus on your first (most crucial task) and work through them. If you have any task left then move them to tomorrow's six tasks and repeat.

"A day can slip by when you're deliberately avoiding what you're supposed to do"- Bill Watterson

Exam Stress & How To Handle It

Everyone has had exam chills. The morning before an exam our abdomen is filled with terror and trepidation. Arriving at the exam hall, our feet tremble in anguish as it can't transport the heavy load of pressure. We place our derrière on our designated seat and wait for the sound of the agonising smarting pricking painful papers being stacked on our desk in front of us by the merciless exam invigilator. Looking around seeing everyone calm causing you to gulp irresistibly.

But how can we prevent & treat this common problem;

Firstly, you must understand such feelings of anxiety and stress are a part of life. Some stress is good for us but when it exists for a prolonged period of time, it can become a burden to our health.

Stress is your body's reaction to a challenge (feeling of threat/pressure). Low levels of stress can actually be good for us in helping to keep us motivate and perform better in certain scenarios. Hormones are released, which results in physical manifestations of stress. These can include slowed digestion, shaking, tunnel vision, accelerated breathing and heart rate, dilation of pupils, and flushed skin. This is known as the" fight or flight response".

Common causes of stress:

- Social acceptance – Making friends and trying to avoid bullying
- Earning good grades - Classes are getting more challenging and they know it's going to be tremendously difficult to get int university with average grades
- Preparing for university – the whole process of picking a subject, writing a personal statement, and attending the interviews can be very tense and stressful.
- Parental pressure – Parents often put heaps of pressure on their teens to encourage them to work harder but this potent force of pressure dumped on their child can have a bad impact.

Note: Stress and anxiety can both occur at one time or another. Stress is a response to a challenge and anxiety is a reaction to the stress

Now that we understand some of the causes, let's dig deeper into exam stress in particular and how we can cope with it

1. **Meditation** - thought the day we encounter stress and our bodies react with the usual fight or flight response. Prolonged stress as we mentioned previously can cause physical damage to every part of the body. The action of meditation enables your body's relaxation response to be trigged. It can calm your mind and body by quieting the stress and shrugging it off enabling ourselves to be tranquil. The Daily Telegraph reported that "after meditation training of 20 minutes once a day for only five days, people, had measurably less anxiety and lower levels of the stress hormone cortisol".
The papers said that levels of anxiety, depression, anger, and fatigue had also gone down.

2. **Eat, sleep, and exercise well** - Pulling all-nighters will not just leave you drained come exam day but will reduce your ability to recall information and study effectively. Exercise gets your blood following and your heart pumping. It fills your brain with endorphins (happy hormones) which are proven to make you feel jubilant and less stressed. Sleep and exercise are both crucial during the exam period but so Is eating the right food as this can have a delightful impact on your mental health and wellbeing.

3. **Believe in yourself** - You will face challenges. You fill face days where you are on 3% and you don't have a charger to empower you. Belief and discipline will be your only saviour on these days. Replacing pessimism with positivity. Know that you have given it your all, you have prepared well and there is no reason why you should worry. instead of thinking 'If I don't get at least an A*, I am a failure', think 'Whatever I get, I will be proud of myself and value how much I have already achieved'. If you don't believe in your capability to succeed no one else will so have faith in yourself.

"If you hear a voice within you say, 'you cannot paint,' then by all means paint, and that voice will be silenced."- Vincent Van Gogh

Advice from students:

"*Looking over some past exam questions or even answering some in exam conditions can help calm your nerves.*"

"*Remember that you're not a machine. You deserve time off! Make sure you factor in time to watch a film, go out for a drink with friends or grab a coffee. The most productive brains are those that rest properly too!*"

"*Break up your revision with some exercise! Whether it's a brisk walk or a session in the gym, not only will it let your mind relax for an hour, you'll also get a burst of energy.*"

"*Do work at home, I can't stress this enough. I regret not starting early.*"

"*When you revise, no distractions. Have a drink on hand and make sure you have enough sleep. Nothing worse than wanting to collapse at your desk.*"

"*Organisation is also key! A ring binder for each subject, constantly updated and kept neat will make revision so much easier.*"

"*Work but don't overwork yourself! Please take off time to relax!*"

About the Author

The author writes all his books intending to provide teenagers with every resource they would ever need to achieve their dream grade. The author knows how distressing and blood- shrieking exams could be therefore he has taken the initiative to change the lives of many hoping to make a better Britain and a better future for many. The author's main intention was to get more children into the courses they want but to also provide resources for every child especially those who can't afford the expenses of tuition. He believes by allowing and supporting more teenagers to getting the top grades with little effort through certified techniques that teachers are unaware of, will hopefully allow them to pursue their dream careers.

If you find any mistakes in the book then please send me an email: edumap.987@gmail.com

You can find more practice questions and resources on my website www.edumap.org.uk and my Instagram @edumap.official

Editor: Tom

Author: Ahmaan Immo

Printed in Great Britain
by Amazon

17820963R00043